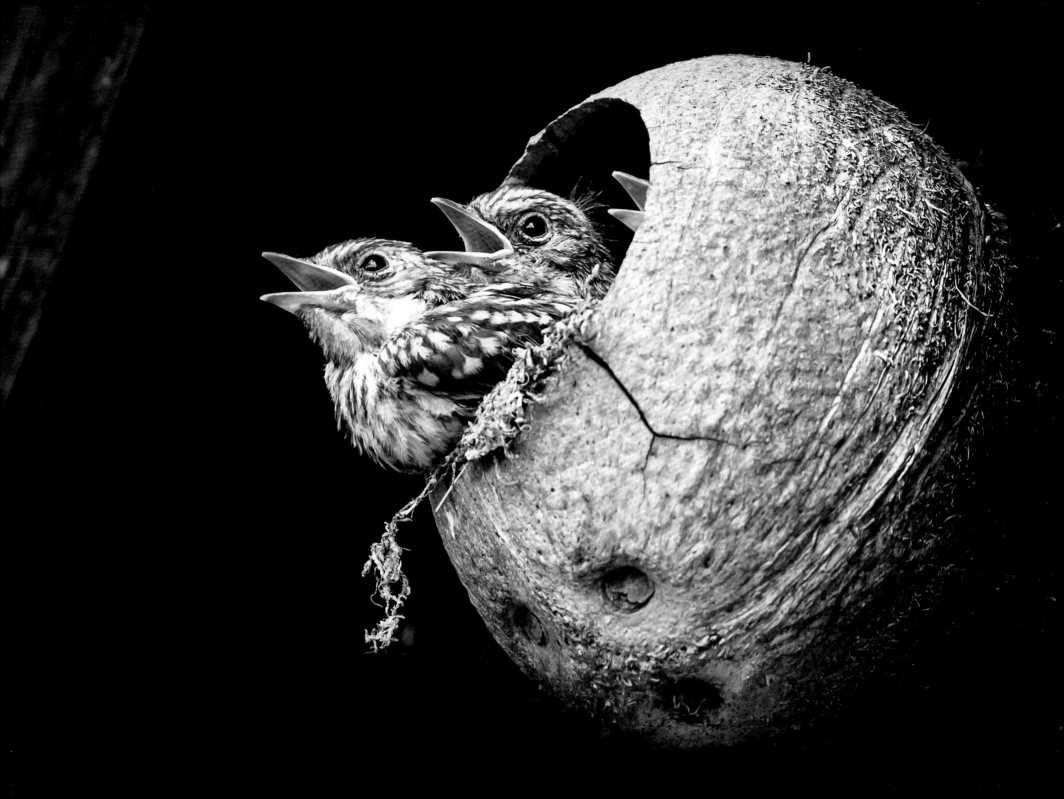

HILL & DALE
MY SHROPSHIRE YEAR
ANDREW FUSEK PETERS

HILL & DALE

Over hill, over dale, Thorough bush, thorough briar,
Over park, over pale, Thorough flood thorough fire.
—'A Midsummer Night's Dream', Act 2, scene 1

Here be hill that cradles dale
The basking adder's curling tail;
Here be dew and dragonfly
And egret under snowy sky;
Here be hare to suckle young,
And singing thrush, her tiny tongue
With finch and fieldfare symphony
The little owl accompany.
When the rain-racked rivers rise,
Sudden salmon take to skies,
Flooded fields a city-nation,
Rush-hour rippling murmuration.

Here be woods and damson night,
And dawn where softened mists alight.
Listen, for the dusk's in tune;
Take note of silver, chiming moon,
And later, in the deeps of dark,
Each star a solemn, singing lark
And breathing in the shadowed wood
The fallow sleeping as they should
As up above, that bird of prey,
The perching, perfect Milky Way.

Here be promise, here be song;
Come ye faithful, come along!
To nature's harvest let us reap.
For still it's not too late to keep
The promise of the butterfly,
The call of wren to amplify:
Shropshire, where my heart shall spill
Through hill and dale and dale and hill.

Milky Way and Perseid meteor, Long Mynd; little owl.

CHASING THE LIGHT

I fell in love with Shropshire as a young man when I met my wife-to-be, Polly, who had spent her teens under Ragleth Hill. Most Friday nights after work she would drive me to her mother's house in Little Stretton. We headed up Small Batch onto the Long Mynd where a steep climb brought us to the source of the stream. To my urban eyes, this spot was a murmuring miracle. At the very last minute, we pulled out of buying our first house in Bristol and found instead a new home in Bishops Castle. We have never looked back.

I took up photography in 2013 after twenty-five years of work as a children's author. I was burnt out and had no idea that the opening of a third eye could fill me with new vision and purpose. I had walked these hills and explored these valleys but the camera added focus and passion. With wildlife there came a deep and abiding love and respect. I built relationships with landowners and conservation bodies such as the National Trust and Natural England, for whom I have been working on a long-term commission documenting the flora and fauna of the Long Mynd and the Stiperstones [explored in my previous book *Upland* and my *National Trust Guidebook to the Long Mynd*].

My fellow Salopians have opened their hearts and their local secrets to me. This journey of discovery has uncovered a miscellany of tales: the deer who thinks he's a cow; the white egret in the blizzard; the ultra-rare leucistic red kite residing on a Stiperstones farm, and the roosting black darter dragonfly on the Mynd silhouetted by a golden sunset. I have grabbed the light of dawn and the light of dusk and beyond them the moon and the Milky Way. Above all, I have celebrated these Shropshire hills and dales and hope to continue my close-to-home safari for many years to come.

Through intense study of behaviour, years of fieldcraft, the use of a completely silent and small camera setup, a mobile hide, long lens and/or remote control, I have been able to achieve close-up shots while being a respectful distance away. In my work with wildlife I always put consideration for the species first. I am constantly amazed at how wildlife co-exists with humans: nesting in trees overlooking busy roads and paths; making homes in gardens, in cottage walls next to front doors, even on the hinge of a much-used allotment door. Such proximity still requires great care. My aim is to show intimate moments while always being immensely careful about disturbance. By sharing such beauty, I hope to make people think about conservation and about what we are in danger of losing.

Four-spotted chaser at sunset, Long Mynd; leucistic red kite, Stiperstones.

Road-injured hawfinch picked up and taken to Cuan Wildlife Rescue; kingfisher with fish; honeybee in lavender at Stokesay Court; red admiral in flight; singing wren.

JANUARY
WAKING IN THE DARK HOURS

The year begins with both flight and flourish. It has now been statistically proven that putting out feeders in your garden in the cold months makes a huge difference. The goldfinch used to be a bird of the farmyard and as a species had begun to decline dramatically. But our love of wildlife outside the window, and the provision of winter fuel, has seen goldfinch numbers begin to rise again. How wonderful that January can deliver a good news story.

I can't complain when goldfinch, due to its feisty nature, faces off against a very colourful siskin. It reminds me of childhood playground squabbles. Using our kitchen as a hide, I am photographing through double-glazed glass, trying to catch a moment that seems faster than the blink of an eye. When the snow comes, the goldfinch even faces off against the brute force and size of the bigger chaffinch. What a marvel of light that the individual snowflakes are caught mid fall.

It's worth waking in the dark hours and driving through the sleepy lanes up the back of Caer Caradoc. A shortish climb as the pre-dawn light fills out the sky and the effort is decidedly worth it. To the east, a volcanic outcrop called the Battle Stones rears up from Willstone Hill.

Myths say one of the great battles between the Romans and Britons in AD51 took place here though historians now dismiss this. It is nevertheless a wonderful sight and sets off superbly the sun rising behind the distant Brown Clee Hill.

Goldfinch holding its ground against the chaffinch; siskin and goldfinch squaring off.

Battle Stones at dawn; dawn over the Mynd.

There are plenty of buzzards in South Shropshire but they are the shyest of birds. I merely have to sneeze five miles away and they are guaranteed to fly off. They have also adapted incredibly well to our countryside infrastructure and particularly to our telegraph poles, which possibly appear to them as a sort of denuded tree with a satisfactory perch. Even better, their feathers match the colour of the telegraph pole so that I sometimes have to look twice before I realise that yes, that is a buzzard doing its thing. To catch their take-off reveals the incredible intention of flight. Even better, in the rich orange dusk light, I manage to frame a pair of buzzards swooping low under the branches of a distant tree. Like sleek shadow-puppets, they vanish into the evening.

I see movement in the field and realise it's two hares spooked by the buzzards. They are keeping low, with only their ears to give them away.

There used to be plenty of lapwing in South Shropshire, but that was before much of the farmland was drained for productivity after the war. Their numbers are now perilously low. Even to see this small flock flaring up over farmland near Church Stretton feels like a glimpse of former beauty. The one spot we do get good winter numbers is Venus Pool near Shrewsbury. When a lapwing poses for me in good light, I can see the iridescent sheen of its wings and its dainty feather arrangement.

Buzzards flying in to roost at dusk; hares; buzzard take-off.

Lapwings near Stretton; lapwing at Venus Pool; coots dancing on ice.

When the morning mist comes, I drive up to Edgton and see the Shropshire Hills open up in front of me. Ragleth Hill and Caer Caradoc rear out of the mist. Dawn breaks through in a single finger of light, stretching across the panorama like a painting.

At Walcot, the lake has mostly frozen over. I decide rather foolishly to lie down in the snow on the bank to get at eye-level with a pair of uncertain coots. They are not in favour of slippery ice, but their careful steps give me a delightfully synchronised dance movement. Definitely worth a chilly half-hour!

The goosander are shy as ever. The moment I point my long lens in their direction, they are off, almost sliding over the lake's solid surface. On the far bank which the ice has not yet reached, the little egret appears to resemble the clumps of snow behind it. I hope it was successful in finding a fishy snack.

The snowdrops are out at last and the snowfall reveals crystalline treasure. I have to rush up the lane to get to the snowdrops before the sun warms them. With my macro lens, and 'focus stacking', I capture my first ever snowflake, perched precariously on the snowdrop's flank. I am stunned by the intricate detail.

Goosander flying over the ice at Walcot; little egret in the snow; snowflake on a snowdrop. [Next pages: the view to Ragleth and Caradoc as the morning light breaks through.]

At this time of year, with the sun much lower in the sky, there is the chance of intense and colourful sunsets. I race over to the Stiperstones on a hunch.

The wind has dropped and the forecast is good. I can feel the anticipation as I park and begin the walk up towards Diamond Rock. I am so honoured to have been commissioned to work on this nature reserve for the last few years. I have never had a dull visit yet, but this evening is exceptional. All is bathed in glory.

The sunset flares off the quartzite outcrop like a golden star, and when the crescent moon rises over Manstone Rock, the dusk fills my heart with hope.

On evenings such as this, it's good to be alive.

To say that I am passionate about the moon would be an understatement. As I come back from a shoot one evening, I spot it rising above our garden. I can also hear and see a little song thrush singing in my neighbour's tree. I wonder if I can line up the two.

I run round the inside of the house and finally end up climbing onto the roof of the conservatory, hoping the thrush won't fly away. I feel both blessed and lucky as I get bird and open beak framed by the golden circle of the rising moon.

There is another sign up our lane of new beginnings. In the hollow of the old oak tree in the middle of a vast field, barn owl is sunning itself, a white extravagance among rich brown bark.

Sunset over Diamond Rock; thrush singing at moonrise.

Bittern in flight; nuthatch; female blackbird with berry; a barn owl's perfect fit! [Next pages: Manstone Rock and the crescent moon; moonset over the Devil's Chair.]

January ends on an instinct.

For all the years I have been honourably chasing the moon, it has always been at sunset or dusk as the moon rises. However, the moon plays a game of follow-my-leader with the sun, rising in the east and setting in the west, though the timings change throughout the year. I wonder if it's possible to catch moon-fall over the Stiperstones ridge.

This requires a big telephoto lens, some careful calculation and perfect weather.

When Puck girdles round the world and swings the planets in my favour, I find myself zooming over the great whaleback of the Long Mynd way before dawn. The moon is still bright in the dark sky and moving gently in a downward diagonal from left to right. I can feel it in my blood: if I just find the right spot, she will sink right behind the Devil's Chair.

I cannot believe I am alone to witness this, sitting on the cold wet ground and watching the moon clip the Needle's Eye. It was said, way back in the nineteenth century, that if you passed a sick child through this hollow gap, they would be made well.

Well, I feel like the first to see this miracle — the wavering yellow moon, distorted through the haze of the atmosphere, shining like a beacon.

What a catch! I give a whoop of joy.

As I drive home, on the other side of the Mynd, the red sun fills the dull valleys and it's time for breakfast.

FEBRUARY
SECRET AND WINDY EVENINGS

February is for foxes. I have been stalking this elusive but stinky mammal all morning under the careful and expert guiding of Tris from Tris Pearce Wildlife. Many of the fields in this part of North Shropshire still retain their ancient hedgerow shapes, a higgledy-piggledy patchwork that means we stalkers can use brush and bramble for cover.

This kind of safari requires a complete camo cover-up, including headgear and dark gloves to hide bright-coloured skin. After three hours, we come upon the territory of an old dog fox that Tris has been following for a few years. The scent is incredible, a perfumed path that lets everyone know who rules this area. Finally, we see movement on the far side of the field and make quietly for the cover of some overgrown bushes. Tris knows his stuff, as there before me is fox, settling down and finally having a kip.

Our disguise, and our being downwind, has worked. I feel both blessed and sad that this is the closest I have got to fox since I started my photography in 2013.

Foxes in North Shropshire.

When one of the local farmers under the Stiperstones tells me he's got a white kite in residence, I have my doubts. Surely it's a (quite common) very pale buzzard? But he insists I come to have a look. This is one of the infrequent moments where he's hit the nail on the head. In the valley above the farm, as I pull over and park up, I see a white blob in a distant tree.

My lens confirms this is something out of the ordinary, something that indeed sticks out of the landscape. Over two days, I photograph this bird, still unsure what I am seeing until I confer with ornithologist and conservationist Leo Smith.

The leucistic red kite is a genetic aberration that occurred first when the last remaining UK population, in Wales, was down to only a few breeding pairs in the 1990s.

Due to inbreeding, an ultra-rare genetic anomaly arose and it was this — a kite with pale markings, very broken and tatty tail feathers, and generally sterile.

At the time I photographed it, it was one of only a handful of birds recorded in England, with a tamer pair at Gigrin kite-feeding station.

Thanks to huge conservation efforts, including bringing kites over from Spain and Scandinavia, the kite population has recovered and is slowly spreading back to its old haunts.

I see this bird for two days and then never again. What an honour to witness such wonder.

Leucistic red kite in farmland under the Stiperstones, and with a crow. Compare with red kite, top right on previous page.

At Walcot Lake on a cold and grey afternoon, the alpha male swan is acting like a bully once more. When it goes for lesser males, it does it with brutal gusto, and such behaviour is strangely known as 'busking'. Brutal is the right word, as victims can often end up banished to the bank of the lake to starve to death.

On the heights of the Stiperstones and the Mynd, a cold-weather specialist is ignoring icy February winds. Red grouse are no longer hunted on these two nature reserves, except by this photographer keen for a pretty picture.

Red grouse have feathers going right down to the claws on their toes. They use heather for cover but are quite adept at surviving altitude like their cousin the ptarmigan.

Nearby, on upland, new life is already braving the cold to try and begin again. The frogs have laid their spawn high on Nover's Hill and seem willing to risk frost and freeze. I go in at sunset to try and show the spawn lit up inside the pool against the colourful dusk backdrop on the Mynd. Returning before dawn, I catch sunrise over Caer Caradoc and distant Clee.

But for actual frogs, I don't need to go far, as a very sedate frog turns up in a damp garden corner one morning and seems quite happy for me to take a ridiculously close-up shot of its eye. Look carefully and you can see the façade of our old chapel reflected in the catchlight. Who knew that a frog's wide-angle eye can take in more than any camera!

A close-up of a frog on our patio; busking male swan at Walcot Lake.

Red grouse on the Mynd and the Stiperstones.

Mating frogs at Edgton and frogspawn on Nover's Hill. [Next pages: dawn on the Long Mynd.]

This little frog was very obliging as I lay down on the wet ground to catch an intimate portrait.

Kestrel numbers are dropping alarmingly in Shropshire.

In my garden and in the village, we are having some wonderful visitors. Siskins it seems are born squabblers and a few weeks of missed shots eventually lead to some wonderful flare-offs. A little yellow-necked mouse that probably lives in our shed takes advantage of seeds hidden in my Japanese reflecting-pool. On the yew trees in our village churchyard, an influx of hawfinches finally leads to a colourful portrait by a posing male.

Just up the old sunken road which is locally known as Watery Lane, the snowdrops are putting on a good show, reminding us that spring will arrive eventually. In the field behind the snowdrops, I stalk a hare by crawling through the muddy ground, trying to present neither threat nor silhouette. The hare even has a snooze right in front of me, which does make me feel all is well with the world.

A rare yellow-necked mouse; two siskins fighting; hawfinch; long-tailed tit; blue tit and siskin fight; black redstart; time-lapse collage of black redstart in flight.

The month finishes with a story that leads to an unexpected treat. My son lost his wallet in Church Stretton and it was picked up by T who works at the local bakery: this good gentleman worked out who it might belong to, and the wallet was returned.

But that was not all: T, as a keen local photographer, had something to tell me. Having seen an episode of *Winterwatch* where a picture of a treecreeper roosting in a sequoia was shown, T decided to look in the tree on his own patch and he found a feathery miracle. It was even more miraculous that he was willing to share his secret. On a windy evening I got to see treecreeper snuggling up against warm, soft bark. I had to use a long lens so as not to disturb this bird bravely roosting right on a busy driveway in the glare of passing car headlights.

A blue tit in flight; a very relaxed hare; jackdaw against the misty sun Long Mynd.

Snowdrops against the dusk; roosting treecreeper South Shropshire.

MARCH
BEGINS WITH A BLIZZARD

March begins with a blizzard and ends with new life. It is sad that snow is a rarely seen phenomenon these days, because when it arrives it gives a tempestuous flourish. The village and hills around are quickly covered and only the foolhardy would get in a car.

So, as the wind rises and a blizzard blots out background, I feel like the only person alive as I crunch my way to Walcot Lake. The little egret has been in residence over the winter but too shy to let me take a portrait. Now the snow has slowed both the world and this elegant bird; suddenly we are in a Japanese painting as egret drifts through the speckled air. Sad that *egretta garzetta* was almost hunted to extinction: its beautiful nuptial plumes made perfect feathers for Victorian ladies' hats. But out of conservation concern, the Plumage League was formed in 1889.

The League later became the Royal Society for the Protection of Birds, the species was saved and has recently returned to these shores. The birds have slowly been making their way north, and in their slipstream we also have the first ever great white egrets in this area.

What an honour when one takes off in front of me!

Great white egret at Walcot; little egret in the blizzard.

The cold weather also brings the unusual discovery of a barn owl hunting by day.

It is so hungry that it entirely ignores the odd human, me, poking my lens over a hedge in the fields near our village.

This time the owl is unsuccessful, landing on a pile of brash a few feet away. I find owl again by dusk, quartering the fields near the old tennis courts.

Catching the elegance of flight is always enough to make my day.

Meadow pipit on the Long Mynd; barn owl.

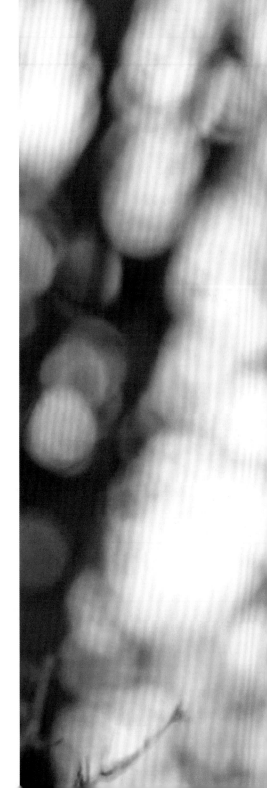

Morning mist on Titterstone Clee Hill; snow bunting in flight while another enjoys a walk on the hill. The star trails are over Titterstone Clee Hill.

51

My neighbour in Brockton has been in touch to tell me of a monster lurking in her stream.

I head over with my underwater system and by the little bridge that crosses from her garden to the fields, I spot a tiny wriggling mass.

My hands freeze as I hold my underwater camera to capture these eel-like creatures clasped onto a pebble.

These ancient life forms, on the Red List of threatened species, have a sucker disc instead of a mouth, with two tooth plates and a few blunt teeth.

It was said that Henry the First died of a surfeit of lampreys, and if I hold my hands in the water any longer, I think I might join him!

To move from macro to massive is part of the joy of my work and I return to that other great upland, the Stiperstones.

A bit of moon-chasing at dusk pays off as I run up the hill, gasping for breath, hoping to catch the supermoon rising behind Manstone Rock. My wildlife telephoto lens brings the moon close – planning and good timing paying off.

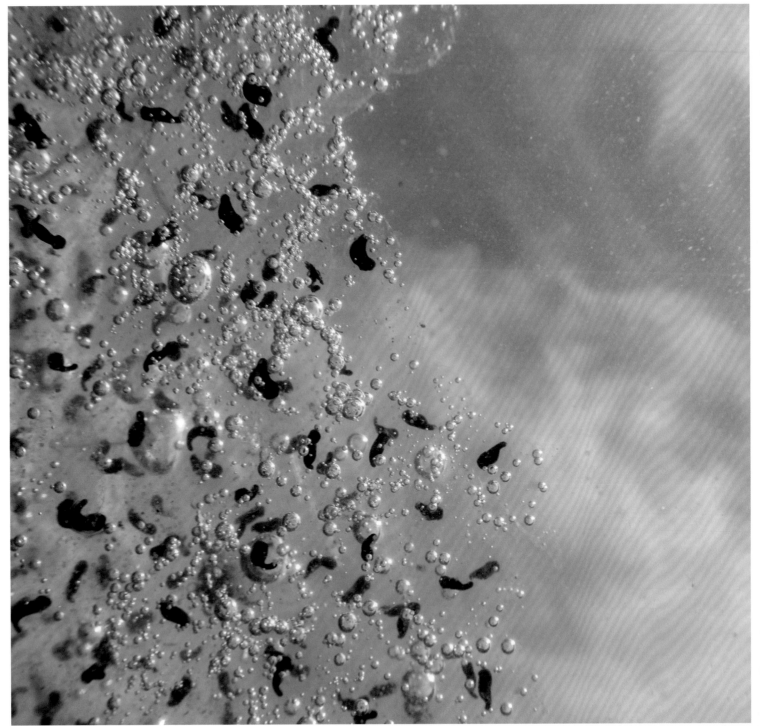

Frogspawn and sky, Long Mynd; brook lampreys at Brockton.

These spring dawns reveal one further watery opportunity.

The online community has recently been awash with rumours of a mammal that vanished almost completely from our once very polluted rivers. With cleaner water, the perfectly adapted fish hunter can be found, if you are lucky, in almost all our Shropshire watercourses, mimicking a national trend.

So far, I have turned up to this particular spot at least three times, haring through the darkness to reach the town as the sun rises, and my only rewards are some geese and good chats with fellow mammal addicts.

But persistence pays off, and at Bridgnorth, in the Severn, as commuters drive and traipse across Low Town Bridge, I catch my first glimpse of sinuous, sleek fur and the grace of a cat, curling into the deeps for food and fuel.

Otter is both marvel and miracle and I am almost shaking with excitement to be so close to such wildlife in the midst of a busy rush hour.

Supermoon rising over Manstone Rock; the Bridgnorth otter.

Having built a little reflecting-pool in my garden, I was rewarded with a blue tit meeting its twin as it flew over the water: two blue tits for the price of one!

Out driving later, a brief flare in the heather reveals a meadow pipit performing a perfect balancing act. Perhaps the commonest bird on our upland, but arrayed like this, not a bird to be sniffy about.

Tree sparrow in the village, Long Mynd; blue tit at the garden pond; meadow pipit on the Long Mynd.

Our neighbour Diana rings up to share some exciting news. A mutual birding friend had been having tea at her house and spotted an interesting bird on the feeders outside her window. What had looked like a small flock of house sparrows hanging out for nosh turned out to be a bunch of much rarer tree sparrows. There is one tree sparrow for every fifty house sparrows and they are sadly declining in number. But here they bounce about the rhododendron with those fabulous black sideburns and chestnut-topped heads, a colourful symbol of spring.

At the end of the month, I get a phone call. My friend Jo has a smallholding at eleven-hundred feet on the Shropshire border. For the last two years, a jill hare has been coming into her garden from the surrounding wilderness. This year, for the first time, she has given birth in the garden and, during the day, hidden her leverets in the flower borders. The hare is used to Jo doing her gardening and is quite tolerant of human activity. There is a chance to catch something rarely photographed – and it requires great patience.

I arrive during early evening and scout the garden, finding one of the leverets tucked into the edge of the kitchen garden. Their survival strategy is to stay still and low. After one photo, I retreat so as not to disturb the young hare, then decide the best place to wait is the kitchen. The light falls, the dusk deepens, and two leverets suddenly shoot out from their hiding places to scamper about the cut grass. A few minutes later and mum turns up. It is so dark I have to shoot at 1/15 of a second, but there, in front of the window, she suckles her young. This behaviour has been captured only a handful of times before, and the feeding lasts just a couple of minutes. Then they are groomed and mum heads off, leaving the leverets to hide in the garden once again.

Leveret in the garden; mother hare feeding two leverets.

Garden birds (brambling, chaffinch, redpoll); dusk at the Knuckle.

APRIL
BIRDS AND BLOSSOM

April begins with both heat and blossom. In the flowering cherry tree that borders the walk to Walcot Lake, the blue tit is busy plucking blossom, perhaps for nectar which is a valuable food source during breeding season.

A few days later, on the hill above our house, the walking of our dog is curtailed by my first-ever sighting of a short-eared owl, carefully quartering the top fields.

Lola is stuffed unceremoniously back in the car as I crouch and crawl among the hedgerows. I am sure that owl sees all, but is not bothered, being glorified in the gilding of sunset. Both my heart and the owl end up glowing in this last light.

Short-eared owl; blue tit in the cherry blossom.

When I see kestrel diving out of the sky high on Titterstone Clee Hill, I ask my friend to stop driving and I leap out of his van. 'Then off, off forth on swing, as a skate's heel sweeps smooth on a bow bend' is how the poet Hopkins described the windhover.

Historically, the aerial acrobat had many rural names: fleingell or fly-in-the-gale, mouse-falcon, stannel or stone-yelled; the jack-hawk in Yorkshire; in Old French, crecerelle. In the first English appearances, the word itself seems to hover about kistrel, kastrel, keshrel before settling in its final form some time in the late seventeenth century.

For once, I catch focus exactly but it is only when I open up my images on the screen that I can see the sequence of kestrel catching a bumblebee, stripping its wings then dropping it, only to dive in order to snatch that last juicy protein morsel. I had no idea they took insects, but when hungry, this efficient hunter is far from fussy.

Hunting is exactly what I witness when my wife shouts, 'Sparrowhawk!' and I manage to frame the moment when it takes a collared dove on our lawn. A few days later, I assume stoat is also grabbing food as it brings in prey to a hole in my neighbour's haystack. It takes some research and helpful feedback to reveal that these embryo-like forms are in fact the young kits being moved to a new den. What a wonderful catch!

Our garden now becomes the site of an avian feeding frenzy. I get busy in the kitchen capturing fight and flight through the double-glazed window.

Back in our garden, the visitors to our feeder show that even regular garden birds have their beauty. To see the flare of robin among the primulas, the brute muscularity of greenfinch and a pair of goldfinches going at it hammer and tongs is a delight.

Kestrel diving for bumblebee; sparrowhawk taking a collared dove; stoat and kits.

Robin flaring up through primula; siskin and greenfinch; a greenfinch with attitude; a great tit landing; goldfinch taken at a slow shutter speed; a pair of fighting goldfinches.

The birds are not just eating but making ready for the next generation. I am suddenly looking up during my walks and realising that holes in the bark contain avian treasure. When I see the female woodpecker emerge from the nest high up in an oak tree, my life suddenly feels full of colour and hope.

The nuthatches are busy grabbing mud from under a cattle grid to make a natural gap in the bark small enough to keep chicks safe. And the blue tit reveals that there is nothing common about that awesome wingspan. Sometimes, a long lens really does the job of getting me in close without bothering these busy birds.

Blue tit flying from hole; nuthatch, great spotted woodpecker and blue tit emerging from their nests.

The orange-tips are some of the first new butterflies to emerge and I spend a ridiculous amount of time running up and down verges, chasing these flighty beauties. It's worth it though when they settle down to mate. Patience also finally pays off when I catch a male taking off from a bed of forget-me-nots.

At dusk, I lie down in the nettle-filled verge to capture a roosting green-veined white against the yellow afterlight. A green thought in a green shade, indeed.

Orange-tip in flight; mating orange-tips; green-veined white at dusk; orange-tip against the yellow disc of a dandelion flower.

Slow-worms and adders used to be incredibly common in the UK, but both have declined and it takes help from a friend and a thorough search of verges on the edge of Clun to unearth a slow-worm that looks like a small smooth twig. Reptiles love to bask in sunny April days and when, thanks to the bard of Whixall Moss, Stephen Barlow, I finally see my first adder, I stand at a safe distance and fall a little bit in love. Their ability to stay utterly still rivals that of any patient photographer.

I often pass fields being ploughed and have noticed that the rich brown furrows attract raptors and crows keen on a wormelicious feast. Stephen, who farms at a thousand feet in the hills above Clun, offers to take me out one sunny afternoon. I find myself ensconced in the belly of a huge, rumbling beast where even a tyre costs five hundred quid. Luckily, the tractor is invisible to the visiting buzzards and I frame eye and hungry intent among rich loam.

Buzzard following the plough; adder at Whixall Moss; slow-worm at Clun; dandelion at sunset.

The pied flycatcher family has taken up residence in one of the old nest boxes at Walcot Arboretum, perched right over a very busy footpath. Mum and dad are busy bringing in supplies and this gives me the chance to catch them on the wing. The male is strikingly black and white, but the female with wings spread shows a wonderful elegance. I return for a striking dawn at the end of the month. The lake is burnished with golden light and as the mist burns off, we move deeper and more hopefully into the spring.

Pied flycatchers at the nest box; a swan at dawn on Walcot Lake.

MAY
COLOUR AND LIFE

May is the time of newborn colour and life.

A fellow owl enthusiast has told me about his good friends in Bishops Castle whose garden is hosting a pair of tawny owls and their chicks. This site is a seventies bungalow right next to the main road going out of town. In the middle of the lawn is a very convenient hollow tree stump about ten feet tall.

I love the adaptation of tawnies to town life. The switching on and off of lights, the buzz of street lamps, the grumble of complaining lorries inching past: none of these deters the urge to breed. The retired couple who own the bungalow also welcome their tall visitor with camera in hand, searching out hidden youngsters' eyes among recently unfurled copper beech leaves. As dusk comes on, the chicks huddle like a pair of ... well ... of wise owls. Their wrinkliness is not a good indicator of age!

Tawny chick pair at dusk; Helmeth Wood bluebells. [Next pages: sunset over the Devil's Chair.]

I spend almost two weeks visiting, watching the tawny owls roosting by day in the big tree overlooking the road. Just at the point I feel that I might have taken up too much of my friends' hospitality, I am delivered hot, sweet tea on a tray, with crumpets and home-made jam. The good life! Dusk sets in and a chick waits on the bungalow roof for his feast of the evening's worms.

In a cottage on Corndon Hill, redstarts have returned, to use a tiny hole in the wall by the front door. The female is on feeding and poo-carrying duty today. I set up my silent equipment and retreat to the far side of the garden with a remote control. I am hoping to catch a wide-angle context moment to show wall and door, garden flowers and sky. After three hours of missed shots, the sun comes out, and I love the way the colour of the flaring female, off to get more nosh, matches the door.

Closer to home, an old friend has put me in touch with a landowner whose hedge-bound, ancient oak tree hides a hollow secret. All they have seen these last few years is a blur of flight and flurry of feathers, but they are pretty sure a pair of little owls is in residence. This nineteenth-century French migrant was deliberately introduced by wealthy landowners, and has adapted quite well to our landscapes and seasons.

I gain permission to put a hide near the tree and months of work begin. Little owls, like most wildlife, are intelligent and sensitive to their surroundings. Walking in with a camera and long lens generally triggers a flight response. Consideration is called for but the owls quickly get used to the hide that has popped up in the field. I spend many hours in the hide practising the art of quiet patience. It is an amazing experience to simply be in nature.

A hare comes up and feeds almost right by me, and the crows as ever do their best to hassle the local buzzard. Finally, it takes a very early start long before dawn. I creep through the field and edge myself into the hide. The golden dawn creeps up the bark, turning a dull tree into a shining jewel, topped off by little owl popping out on its perch, grabbing the first rays of the morning sun and providing me with a perfect portrait.

I have gone on a half-day holiday to my neighbour's garden. It's worth the visit as I become interested in a bird I would never have thought to photograph. House sparrows are aptly named, as a pair has nested in a disused kitchen vent. To say they are relaxed around humans would be an understatement! One female chick is sticking her head out; all are ready to fledge. Sparrows have declined alarmingly in the last forty years and

are now on the Red List. When they fly out of the nest they are far from dull, but reveal their own concise elegance.

As I wander round the garden, I hear a very loud song from the vicinity of a holly and realise to my amazement that the dainty wren, who weighs no more than a pound coin, is building a nest among all those sharp leaves, a green armoured fortress. I love the contrast of soft white feather lining and prickly bush.

Wren with feather; house sparrows living up to their name. [Next pages: tawny chick hiding in the copper beech; female redstart leaving nest.]

Woodpecker chicks make a chit-chit-chit sound as they call for food and it's the perfect homing beacon for both flying parents and keen photographers. They seem to love carving their nests right above busy public footpaths which means I can set up remote control and retreat to a safe distance. The chick is easily identified as it has a red cap on its head. The nest hole has often been chipped away, revealing a reddish edge around the bark and is perfectly sized for adults to squeeze through. I love the colour of a great spotted woodpecker but also admire the way it creeps round trunks and is surprisingly hard to spot. The birding gods are with me this year as I have spotted five nests so far and am glad that this vibrant bird is doing so well.

Great spotted woodpeckers.

The end of May is worth the wait. Up in Helmeth Wood under Caer Caradoc, the bluebells have burst into the undergrowth like welcome strangers, so much colour lounging around among the greenery. And nearer to hand, in a private wood of a friendly farmer, I have finally been able to read the map before me. In a place where there are no footpaths, why are the bluebells trodden down in a curving, ancient line?

Ask fox or badger, deer and hare and they might tell you they have their own mammalian songlines, criss-crossing dawn and dusk, radiating out through the night as we sleep. I have the absurd idea that if I sit by the path long enough, the hares might come to visit.

Sometimes, dreams come true. I spot three hares running by. It requires a little patience and perhaps a prayer, if that could be appropriate among the trees. For hare's eyesight is not good and if you are still, you can be mistaken for a bush and hare lollops by so close you cannot fit her into the frame.

This is the true magic of May.

86

Little owl in the hollow of an oak tree at dawn; a male redstart feeds his young.

I have wanted to capture the sun setting over the Devil's Chair on the Stiperstones for some years and tonight is the night. The recent cloudless weather helps, as does working out exactly where the sun will set on my 'sun and moon' app. I am using a long lens and I am on the Long Mynd, just over two miles away as the crow flies. As the sun dips down, the sky turns red and the sun is yolk-yellow. Later, as I put the sequence up on screen, I can see a tiny standing figure. It looks like they are holding up the sun! After submitting the pics to my press agency, I wake up on Saturday morning to find my photo has made the cover of *The Times*. How exciting, and what an honour!

Tawny owl fledgling takes a first flight; hares in May.

JUNE
SEASON OF NEW BIRTH

Sometimes I go on safari in my own back yard.

One early June afternoon, we get home and park, and my son points out that we have a robin nesting in the heather on the stone garden wall. This is extreme avian tolerance as the nest is right next to the back of the car. I spend the next few days sitting on my neighbour's verge on the other side of the road, trying to catch the moment when the parents bring worms for hungry mouths.

I go away for a couple of days and on my return find the chicks are fledged and taking short flights around the garden and on the road. The parents carry on feeding them; there is nothing prettier than a fluffed-up robin chick begging for food.

Where we live yields more treasure, as a pair of spotted flycatchers has decided that the tiny niche in the wall of our house above the electric meter is perfect for new life. The insect fuel that the parents supply grows larger and larger until they are delivering ringlet butterflies and emerald damselflies.

Robin fledglings: one beginning to use its wings, and another being fed by a parent.

Our roof is a pop-up restaurant for the fledgling swallows. I perch precariously on the edge of my son's treehouse and hope for the moment of elegant airborne delivery. I now consider our cosy old chapel to be its very own miniature nature reserve.

Everywhere, the season of new birth bears fruit. The little owls, perfectly ensconced in their old oak tree, have delivered two inquisitive fluffball chicks. They blend into the bark with ridiculous ease and as I walk into the field they are curious rather than nervous.

At my friend Tom's house in Kempton, the blue tits are nesting in a bright blue ceramic box that is right next to their laundry lines. I have an idea for a picture that later possibly reveals I am going through my artistic blue period: blue sky, blue laundry, blue pegs, blue nest box, blue reflections in the gutters and blue tit flying the nest. It feels like an achievement to reveal such colourful wide-angle wonder.

At the same spot, Tom has taken inspiration from William Cobbett's *Rural Rides*, and affixed a scallop shell underneath the eaves. It's a clever foundation on which the house martin builds its nest – a home for the summer until parents and young migrate back to sub-Saharan Africa.

Spotted flycatcher with ringlet butterfly; swallow feeding on our roof; a feast of worms; flycatcher with a damselfly. [Next pages: blue tit; little owl chick.]

A few cloudy days take me to Walcot Lake where the wind has dropped and the surface of the water is both strange and still. One swan has no idea it is drifting along with a perfectly reflected *doppelgänger* and finally, after twenty-five years of walking here, I witness a cygnet having a ride on mum's back.

What I look for is an unexpected intimacy and sometimes that requires putting up a hide in my friend's garden. I make a final visit to meet Jo's mother hare. Hares in the wild can live up to four or five years, so the fact that she has returned with her young again is an honour of the highest order. It takes a few evenings of sitting in my hide, and yes, with a pee-bottle, as I wait for hours falling into the dusk. The last thing I want to do is stand up suddenly and exit for the loo.

Patience pays off when the jill hare comes in to feed. Hilariously, a grazing rabbit decides to defend its territory and launches into the air, much to the amusement of the hare who ignores such miniature bravado. A few minutes later, the nervous leveret comes scooting out from the long grass, and once again I witness the miracle of mother and child right in front of me on the newly cut lawn. They are a matter of feet away from me and I am glad of my silent shutter. I pray my beating heart does not betray me. After a few minutes of mother's milk, she flips baby over and gives her a quick grooming. I can't believe my eyes, as this behaviour has rarely been photographed before.

There are always surprises, and despite the fact that my vision is getting worse with age, in some ways it has sharpened a wildlife-aware edge. This mostly happens when an element in the landscape appears not to fit, be it still or moving.

House martin feeding chick.

As we drive out of the village, I suddenly shout at my wife to stop: 'What's that in the verge?'

It's pouring with rain and a mammal that numbers some thirty million (but is almost never seen) is tracking through the long grass. It's a rather small mole, and, heading for the road, will almost certainly be squished. Their eyes have evolved, or rather devolved, to tiny, unnecessary pinpricks, as most of its senses are located in its bristly nose. Who needs sight underground? We turn it round and hope it finds its way, later finding out that such above-ground excursions are quite common for young moles seeking new territory or to avoid a rising water-table.

My friend Terry has alerted me to a green woodpecker nest on the edge of Church Stretton. This bird is much shyer and rarer than its cousin the great spotted woodpecker and I love its distinctive yaffle laugh which has given rise to its many regional names – yappingale, laughing Betsey, Jack Eikle and nicker pecker. It's worth rising at dawn to set up my remote control and move my chair some distance off so as not to disturb the growing family. Patience is rewarded as mum and dad fly in and out to feed the chicks and take away poo. A green wonder among green leaves!

Everywhere, as the month ends, the landscape is filled with echoes of what was. Foxgloves are an indicator of former afforestation and I like to think of the far side of the Long Mynd before it was so heavily grazed, as a deeply sloping, secretive woodland.

I have returned to the nuthatch nest in time to catch another feeding miracle as both parents fly in and out with insect goodies.

A very rare sight: a hare suckling her young; a very bonkers bunny; three shots of hares & leverets, grazing, hiding & grooming. [Previous pages: swans on Walcot Lake.]

Mole on a mission; a trio of butterflies in flight: green hairstreak, small pearl-bordered fritillary (covered in pollen), dark green fritillary on Stiperstones. 103

The yaffle or green woodpecker; a forest of foxgloves, Long Mynd.

JULY
BLUE SKY AND BEAUTY

July starts with a soaring song.

Curlew have declined dramatically in our Shropshire uplands, but sterling conservation work is slowly bearing fruit. The farm I have patiently worked on for two years yields both blue sky and beauty in the calling curlew as it flies overhead. I spoke to John Sankey, whose family has farmed here for generations and he remembers after the war the boggy land being knee-deep in curlew and peewit.

The song of the Stiperstones is also present at dusk on the Devil's Chair, when rich ruby is the colour that adds harmony to the landscape.

At the Bog, among the old mine workings, the common blue butterflies settle to roost in the long grasses, and I lie down in the stony warmth, trying to catch butterfly against the ripe yellow backdrop of sunset. They are named not because they are common but for the fact they are of the commons.

Calling curlew under the Stiperstones; the Devil's Chair at dusk.

The Flower Garden at Stokesay Court has yielded another miniature treasure. As a cut-flower business, their bed of lavender transforms into a purple landscape while honeybee goes about its work. The small tortoiseshells also flit about and I finally catch my first ever butterfly flight shot. This walled garden was derelict for many years, so it's lovely to see this hidden spot filled with lavender, orange-wonder snapdragon and all things colourful for summer weddings.

I am on a butterfly roll now, and head across the border into Worcestershire to find a species I have never seen.

Penny Bank is a wildflower meadow on the slopes above Martley, a vibrant flower haven that contrasts the main road which runs below it. As I walk through the gate, I see my first ever marbled white, and the description is totally apt.

I venture to the far north of Shropshire, chasing sightings of the rare silver-studded blue. At Prees Heath, bounded by main roads, if one looks closely among the bell heather, there are butterflies in their thousands. Great conservation work at this former RAF airfield has paid off and sunset is the perfect time to photograph these beauties.

Small tortoiseshell; honeybee among lavender at Stokesay Court; silver-studded blue at sunset among bell heather, Prees Heath; female common blue at sunset, the Bog. 109

Bury Ditches is one of the few strongholds of the wood white butterfly in the Midlands. Careful conservation work and many volunteer hours have seen the habitat improved and numbers rise.

On a cloudy afternoon, I head up to the Long Mynd and the flushes below Pole Cottage. To my great surprise, the normally flighty whinchats pose perfectly among the ferns. The bulky chick calls for food and at sixty frames per second the camera catches dad during take-off. Whinchat numbers halved between 1995 and 2008 and they are now on the conservation Red List. I hope this family makes it back to Africa.

Mating silver-studded blue, Prees Heath; marbled white in flight, Martley; a pair of roosting wood whites, Bury Ditches.

Black darter against a rising moon; ovipositing golden-ringed dragonfly, Long Mynd; six-spot burnet moth near Craven Arms; emerald damselfly at sunset, Long Mynd

July has a final few tricks up its sleeve as I return over several days and evenings to the Long Mynd.

I walk up the tiny path behind the reservoir. The golden-ringed dragonfly is an indicator of good upland health and this is the first time I have seen a female laying eggs. Here is new life in the making and with all our news of ecological disaster, a small good-news story to buck the trend.

At sunset, and with the midges to keep me company, I find a roosting female emerald damselfly and work hard to align insect and falling sun.

On a warm evening in our village, I take our Westie Lola for a walk. On a footpath away from the ancient church, she starts sniffing the ground and straining at the leash. Dashing along in the dusk is a very young hedgehog. It seems to know where it is going.

I have no camera, only my phone, and the dog is very keen to supplement her supper. I lie down on the ground to get an up-close shot and pray no other dog owners are out and about. Dogs are one of the main dangers to hedgehogs.

Male whinchat flight sequence, with (inset) a whinchat fledgling; hedgehog in our village at dusk.

It is worth staying out till after dark, winding my way back off the hills to Bridges and the pub car park. I'm thirsty, but not for a drink, as I am still chasing the light even at this blue hour. The noise of Friday night fills the air with raucousness as I walk very slowly up the lane that leads back to the main road. I study the verges, hopeful for a brightness in the greenery. There! A green glow in the grass, a tiny, enticing lightbulb as the female glow-worm sends out a welcoming signal to attract a male. The council have been persuaded not to cut the verge until later, and such an action, or lack of it, has been a life-saver for this dwindling rarity.

On another clear evening, the nearly full moon rises when there is still light in the sky. The black darter dragonflies have settled on the soft rushes and one female stands out, her stillness allowing me to frantically work settings and focus until I have the shot of the year: black darter against the rising moon. Later in the month, as the new moon means no moon, the sky above Pole Cottage and the bog pool at the back fills with stars and I attempt my first Milky Way panorama.

It is sad to see all that yellow in the picture as it is the result of light pollution from Stretton and beyond. The Long Mynd is a designated dark sky discovery site, but it isn't as dark as it should be.

Female glow-worm at Bridges; Milky Way panorama, Pole Cottage, Long Mynd.

AUGUST

BEGINS AND ENDS WITH STARS

August begins and ends with stars.

I have never before been up Titterstone Clee Hill by night and it is a strange and imposing spot. Despite being so remote, I am surrounded by the orange light pollution of nearby towns.

I love the industrial structures up here, so I take the radar station, used for air traffic control, as my focus point for the Milky Way. I am later honoured to see my photo grace the cover of *Amateur Photographer*.

During the warm days, the hills are filled with vibrance and the old mine workings at the Bog under the Stiperstones are a haven for common blue butterflies. This is the time of mating, but later the crescent moon comes out above Corndon Hill, and later still, I have found their butterfly roosting spot.

It's taken two years to develop a technique to frame close-up butterfly and distant stars in one single 'raw' capture, using a mixture of lighting, film-making attachments and much patience. It's wonderful finally to show common blue against heather and Milky Way.

Milky Way over Titterstone Clee Hill radar station; Mitchell's Fold stone circle at dusk.

The local gardens have produced a bumper crop of wildlife this year. A shout from my wife gets me out of the front door, camera in hand, to witness our first ever hummingbird hawk-moth on the valerian.

At our favourite tea-room, Tea on the Way near Clun, a white-tailed bumblebee is nectaring on spiky *Echinacea*. Purple phlox makes a painterly background and I am starting to see what makes me more and more passionate about photography. I want my pictures to be less about the thing, the species, and more about surroundings, context, light, colour, habitat. A return visit to Stiperstones results in a study of orange. The dark green fritillary is a very flighty butterfly and a colourful addition to the area. Finally, after an hour, one settles on a thistle. I have an opportunity to catch take-off and flight.

We have a new visitor to Bury Ditches this year: it's my first ever silver-washed fritillary. I am a sucker for rarity, or as it is called in the butterfly world, aberration. Some females are of a startlingly different colour, a shade of army olive-green called *valezina*.

It's also the first year that the migrant clouded yellow has come to visit Venus Pool near Shrewsbury, hankering after its favourite food-plant, purple lucerne.

Common blue at the Bog under the Milky Way; two shots of a hummingbird hawk-moth; white-tailed bumblebee on *Echinacea*; dark green fritillary flight sequence.

121

A pair of common blue at the Bog; female silver-washed fritillary valezina aberration, Bury Ditches; clouded yellow in flight, Venus Pool; crescent moon over Corndon Hill.

There is also an unexpected guest near to me.

A friend turns up one day and tells me to get my skates on, as there is a deer that thinks he's a cow. I am slightly circumspect but do as I am told and head to the field where this strange occurrence is supposed to be taking place. The report is spot on, as this four-year-old fallow buck appears to have adopted a herd of cows. Or is it vice-versa? Extraordinary. Perhaps he's lost touch with his own herd but here he is grazing alongside cows, walking with them, running alongside them.

When the national papers pick up the story, a deer expert gets in touch and says she has never seen anything like this. At the moment, his antlers are covered in velvet, but a transformation will soon take place.

The fallow deer that thinks he's a cow; house martin leaving the nest, Lydbury North.

The Long Mynd is also a place of transformation. Thanks to patient conservation work, the heather is the best it's ever been. Here, before dawn, a perfect and vast garden of purple. It's an honour to be up this early.

Little can I know that within two years, the effect of global warming, a terrible drought and a warm winter will wipe out over seventy-five percent of the heather, leaving a blasted heath and a patchwork of poor purple.

But for now, I am cradled by this wilderness and in my constant searches for roosting black darter dragonflies, I have struck dewy gold. I am awestruck at how they persist through cold nights, sometimes even August frosts, to end up shivering in the early morning, trying to shake the beaded moisture from their drenched bodies.

As the sun climbs and finally reaches the soft rushes, the darters dry out and take to the wing once more.

The bank holiday is a time of personal persistence. I have been thinking about Mitchell's Fold stone circle and can't even remember when I last came to photograph there. Even better, I can find no photos of the standing stones under the Milky Way and I sense an opportunity to do something fresh.

It takes three nights of mixed sunsets, annoying cloud, the odd visiting night-trippers (possibly literally) but on the last evening, the sky is clear, there is no haze, and above all, no pesky people. When the Milky Way appears, I feel utterly blessed as I work the settings on my camera trying to catch near and far, stones and stars in one shot. What a way to end the month, with a constellation of treasure on my memory card.

Black darters covered in dew, the Long Mynd; and, bottom left, a southern hawker in flight, Walcot.

Black darter at dawn on the Mynd. [Next pages: purple heather before dawn on the Long Mynd; black darter under the Milky Way; Mitchell's Fold & the Milky Way.]

SEPTEMBER

THE SUMMER HAS A FEW FLUTTERING LAST SURPRISES

September is a time of new beginnings, as the lazy days of summer are tucked back into their cupboard. The light softens and I am on the chase again.

A fellow birder has taken pity on me and shared the secret of a wonderful spot for little owls. This particular pair likes nothing better than perching among the forest of run-down buildings on a farm near Craven Arms.

I feel nervous knocking on the door, but permission is quickly granted and once again my car presents a double function. It appears that, to the owl, a keen photographer sitting in a car with the window down is pretty much invisible. I am grateful for the 'second wind' of September sun, a softer showing than the hard-edged heat of August.

So, as evening draws on, I park up next to a ramshackle shed waiting for the action to happen. In this instance, I blink my eye and what was an empty assortment of lengths of wood and old, puzzling nails, is suddenly and beautifully occupied. In my heart, this portrait among the old detritus of the farm is as wonderful as the light rising on the oak tree of May. Even better, the owl is so relaxed that soon a snooze is in order.

As I drive home, happily stuffed with images, a field full of bales grabs my attention, for here is harvested both rainbow and moon, another Salopian bounty.

I have felt the pull of Brown Clee for some time so I've set my alarm for the dark hours and I wend my way through the back lanes to reach the bulk of the hill long before dawn. My night torch picks out the steep path and the only person I am competing with is myself, though I am keen to reach the summit before the sun rises. I climb through thick, chilled mist until I am finally floating above the top, and there, almost too late, is the sun.

I never recommend pointing your camera directly at the sun once it's claimed the day, but mist is a mitigating factor, a filter that turns my final shot into a minimalist painting.

As the fog clears, I look down into the valley and can see that the world is cleaved into half day, half night. Extraordinary to be above this, looking down into light and shadow, hill and vale.

Sunrise on Brown Clee; the fallow buck that thinks he's a cow, in his September antlers.

The summer has a few fluttering last surprises up her sleeve and for once, my commute to work is measured in metres rather than miles. As the warmth of the day gathers round late flowering *Verbena bonariensis* and purple scabious they become a haven for butterflies.

What I am after is more elusive than a pretty portrait. Not matter how hard I try to predict the direction of travel, the butterflies are tricky customers. But a few thousand shots later and one flutter-by has revealed a delicate jade jewellery speckling its underwing. Even better, there is a white marking etched into the underwing in the shape of a comma. Hence the name, as it darts off to carry on harvesting nectar with that impossibly thin curl of a proboscis, a straw-like tube that rolls up when not in use. Because most butterflies diet only on high sugar content flowers, their lives can be measured in weeks, though peacocks, tortoiseshells and commas can overwinter in a state of near hibernation. This September has also seen a huge influx of painted ladies. These migrants from Africa can fly up to thirty miles an hour, and against the backdrop of our garden's last flowering grasp, their flight is a perfect pattern of beauty.

Everywhere up in the hills, harvest is happening and the ploughing transforms fallow to rich brown loam. I am lucky enough to hang out in the tractor with Steven Roberts, whose family has farmed at Purlogue for generations. We are on the top field, easily over a thousand feet and with a view into the rolling hills round Clun. Kites and buzzards are attracted to the turning earth, hoping for a wormy meal or two. From near extinction in the nineties and with much conservation work, bringing over Scandinavian kites to repopulate, the kite has recovered well. And

what a magnificent bird it is, though somewhat shy. Somehow, the colours of its feathers suit the soil.

Another fallow transformation has taken place as the August deer has rubbed the velvet from his antlers and is revealed in all his magnificence as he hangs out with the herd of cows. I even saw him head-butting one in an imitation of rutting behaviour!

The harvest moon is named after the fact that it rises just as the sun sets, so farmers could continue bringing in the harvest under the light of the moon. I have an instinct that tonight will have perfect conditions – clear sky and no haze. I head to High Park on the Long Mynd up a tiny farm road that winds up behind Bridges and finally crawls over the hump of the Mynd to show Caradoc, Clee and the Wrekin spread out below me. Time is tight – I leap out of the car and run to the nearest high point.

Hay bales, moon and rainbow near Stretton; flight of the comma in our garden; painted lady butterfly in flight in our garden; kite take-off during ploughing, near Clun.

A few minutes later and the red moon inches over the edge of Caer Caradoc and then I am properly moon-chasing like a mad thing, sprinting down the hill through the indifferent sheep as I try to line up all that rich ruby colour with an interesting foreground. Here, the blessings begin, for two wild ponies are nuzzling each other while their foal looks on. The setting looks almost staged, with the ponies as pretty and perfect performers. Even better, it turns out that the mare is pregnant.

When the Daily Mail runs the pictures, they come up with a perfect pun. *Harvest Moon, Foal Moon* indeed.

Perhaps, like the butterflies, our souls also take wing as we lay ourselves down in the valley of time. Ancient memorial customs have been revived at Soulton Long Barrow in North Shropshire. This massive stone monument, with a lintel the size of a small truck, is filled with funereal niches and the whole edifice adds a moving statement to the landscape. I have been commissioned to photograph the barrow by night with an impossible hope that the stars might align. Tim Ashton, the owner of the land, is a willing assistant as the dusk deepens and we try to light the interior with candles. Over a long exposure, it's incredible how powerful a single tea light is and most of the evening is spent blowing out the candles one by one, until the last few transform the doorway into a golden threshold. The stars oblige and the Milky Way cantilevers out above the mound as if to provide a path for those seeking solace.

It is said that butterflies are symbols of resurrection and in that case, here has been a month full of hope, flight and celestial delight.

I gave a talk to Rushbury WI where I met the very friendly Shirley Pennington who both owns and grazes Caer Caradoc. It was a double honour to meet one of her sheep in the purple dusk and whose livery, daubed on her fleecy back, was a perfect match to the evening sky.

Just after dawn from the top of Brown Clee; from Caradoc to the Wrekin at dusk.

Two little owls near Stretton; pregnant mare with foal, Long Mynd; foal and parents under the harvest moon, Long Mynd. [Next pages: the Milky Way above Soulton Barrow.]

OCTOBER
AS CLOSE TO A PAINTING AS I WILL EVER GET

The mild October days give a new lease of life to our garden, or rather to its colourful visitors. I have to be both patient and passionate to catch the moments of lift-off.

The honeybee buzzing above *Zinnia* appears to survive among pink perfection. And the carder bumblebee gives me the eye as it hovers above our perennial wallflowers.

The small tortoiseshell is one of our few overwintering butterflies, often found in cool dark spots such as the Victorian brick ice-cellar in the grounds of an old estate. But on sunny autumn and winter days, they will wake up to fly and feed. Lucky that our *Verbena bonariensis* is still in flower and incredible to capture an action sequence which shows agility and wonder.

Many of our migrants have left these shores, but high on the Stiperstones, a young bird has not yet made the journey. I am out with Simon Cooter, the ranger who looks after this reserve, and he has spotted something unusual. A juvenile cuckoo is feeding on grubs and insects in the autumnal whinberry. I crawl through this mini-jungle and the rather fearless cuckoo lets me have an intimate moment. I hope it was successful in flying to Africa.

Coming the other way, from Scandinavia, two wintering crossbills pose for a portrait, high in the branches of a fir tree on Kerry Ridgeway.

Other migrants have been making the impressive return journey from the mid-Atlantic. Like accurate arrows they dart along estuaries and upriver to the very spot they spawned some years before. Although our mainly Victorian and no-longer needed weir system puts up obstacles, *Salmo salar* appears to be both fish and bird. The salar in its name is a happy combination of the Latin words for 'leap' and for 'salt', the salmon leaping back from the salt-water sea. I perch right on the edge of the water and the resulting close-up shows their sleek beauty.

It is a sunny day at Ashford Carbonel that gives the greatest gift. After four years of shooting at this spot, I finally have sunshine, blue sky, bridge, river, male and female salmon, cock and hen, leaping together – a wide-angle wonder.

Honeybee on *Zinnia*; bumblebee on perennial wallflower in our garden; crossbill pair on Kerry Ridgeway.

Juvenile cuckoo on the Stiperstones; cock salmon at Ashford Carbonel; hen salmon; cock and hen salmon leaping. [Next page: painted lady flight sequence.] 145

Deep in the heart of Mortimer Forest, the rutting season has begun. Alan, the Forestry Commission Ranger, has shown me how to blend into the trees. Wear dark clothing, keep downwind and move slowly and quietly. Within these woods is a deer that exists nowhere else in the world. The 'long-haired fallow' was only discovered in 1953 by the ranger at the time, Gerald Springthorpe.

When he sent a pelt for examination by the first ever UK deer conference, the experts thought he was playing a joke and that this was actually a goat. Centuries of in-breeding due to small deer-park populations led to this hairy genetic mutation. The results are spectacular.

My stealthy vigil is rewarded when a young buck drops off to sleep right in front of me. I love the hair pouring out of its ears and what is known in the business as a hirsute pelage. Later, we find an alpha male and his harem — many of the females are long-haired, but the herd is a mix-and-match with normal fallow.

I ask Alan about numbers and he reckons sixty or so. I am blown away and wonder why this worldwide rarity is not better studied and protected.

Small tortoiseshell flight sequence in our garden; overwintering small tortoiseshell, Walcot Hall; long-haired fallow deer amongst a herd of fallow deer in Mortimer Forest. 149

Wild foal at dawn on the Long Mynd; trees at Walcot Lake; heron; stoat.

The mists have returned thanks to wet days and cold nights. From above, our little village vanishes into soft layers. When I rise long before dawn and hare up to the eastern flanks of the Long Mynd, the sky to the north and far Wrekin has distilled all the reds of autumn into the strongest of spirits. It helps that one of the wild ponies is curious about this camera-wielding interloper. This breed is Cwmdale Prefect and is descended from the last of the Welsh pit ponies. Brian Jones is the commoner who has grazing rights for thirty-five ponies and seven foals. They are hardy stock, staying out on the Mynd all year except for the very harshest of winters.

Autumn has finally revealed all its colours at Walcot Lake – not only am I given a rich reflection, but the still day allows me two herons for the price of one. I have been photographing these shy birds at this spot for some years, but I have never seen one take a pike, and a rather large one at that. The stoat on the lakeside path as I head back is the icing on this seasonal cake.

In the last few years, the National Trust has been buying small meadows on the edge of the Mynd, and after some years of conservation, three fields at Jinlye are producing autumnal treasure. The grass hides an incredible array of fungi including some ruby-red scarlet waxcaps. After a few visits, I finally have the sunset I dreamed of, and can match sky and fungi in one frame.

The Mynd has one last trick up its sleeve. It takes a clear night, no wind, headtorches and a long scramble up from Carding Mill Valley to reach Lightspout Waterfall. With my tripod in the stream and over one hundred and twenty long exposures, I want to show the stars rotating around the Pole Star. The result is as close to a painting I will ever get and a great way to finish off the month.

Earthstar fungus in Lydbury North Churchyard; scarlet waxcaps in Jinlye meadows, Long Mynd. [Next pages: star trails at Lightspout Waterfall.]

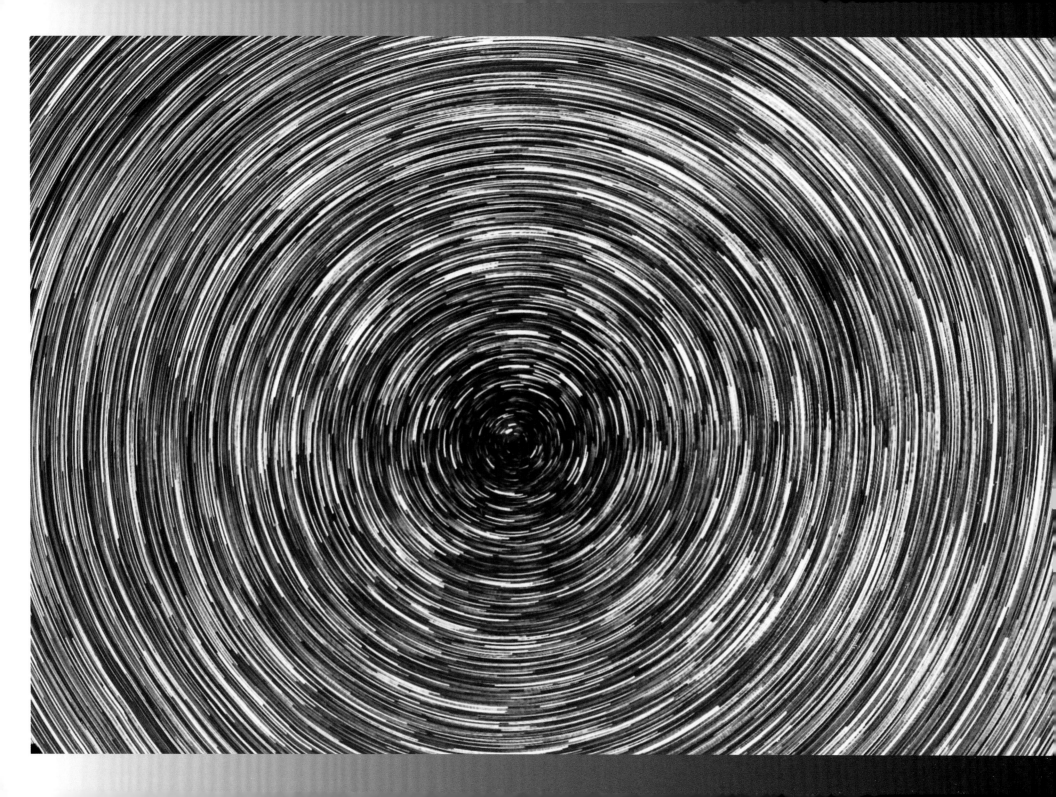

NOVEMBER
THE ECHOES OF SUMMER NOW TRANSFORMED

I am driving back from a photo shoot on the Stiperstones when the sky catches fire. I can see it flaming off to the west, but I'm on a fast road full of bends where it's tricky to stop. I finally find a spot to pull in and the light is like a magnet, drawing me to the place where the day's last embers are burning bright.

I love November and the thick mist that lies gently on the land. The last leaves are hanging on but these trees are already skeletal, their ghosts adorned with the fog that mellows the landscape. This is it, on the side of the A-road as cars rush past, the perfect moment of stillness, the reddening sky like the last hush before winter.

The echoes of summer are now transformed. Battered small tortoiseshells make their way into garages, conservatories and outhouses, and I discover one battling its reflection inside our front window. I put it carefully into cool storage in the dark and come spring, I hope it flutters off to the making of new life. The dandelions are coated in the first hard frost, their softness encased in ice. I wonder whether it would tinkle like a bell if I shook it. When the snow comes, it quickly melts in the valleys, but up in Bury Ditches, among the colouring leaves, a light dusting does the trick.

My friend Rob Rowe is a walking Fungipedia and it is thanks to him that I am quartering Lydham churchyard like an anxious owl, before finally swooping down on purple prey.

I was hoping for something big and spectacular but this clump of ultra-rare violet coral fungi is an unassuming visitor nestled among the gravestones. I am not complaining as a burst of vibrance is just what's needed to dispel the gloomy afternoon blues.

At this time of the year, the lower arc of the sun can set the sky on fire. I am led up the back path through a housing estate on the outskirts of Church Stretton.

Suddenly, we break through the trees onto the bracken-filled slopes of Ragleth Hill. November has worked its charm and rendered a green nuisance into a forest of soft gold. Even better, my middle-aged failing eyes have recently been in training and quickly spot low-slung fungi treasure.

I kneel down to frame oily waxcap and matching dusk light on the Long Mynd's far horizon.

But the sky has the last word on the matter, the very clouds themselves aflame for a few seconds before we descend back into the bosky woods.

Violet coral fungi in Lydham Churchyard; jay with an acorn; dusk over Hyssington.

Frosty dandelion; small tortoiseshell overwintering; snowfall, Bury Ditches; violet coral fungi. [Next pages: sunset from Ragleth Hill; sunset, Long Mynd.]   159

The trees are doing me a favour I am not sure I can repay.

At Venus Pool they backdrop a pleasing flock of curving lapwings. Add in the layering of mist and, closer to home, I feel I am looking down on the far land where a measure of peace is to be had. Within my village and at Walcot Lake, the thrushes and blackbirds are feeding up on berries and seeds before the onslaught of cold. I finally catch my first ever jay in one of the lakeside oaks, a splash of out-there vibrance which makes me feel blessed to photograph a common but shy bird.

A little blue tit leaping about a bush in the warm morning light is the icing on the cake. Why use wings when a quick hop will suffice?

The morning mist in the Kemp valley.

Oily waxcap at sunset on Ragleth Hill; thrush in the yew; juggling blackbird; little egret with fish, Venus Pool; a leaping blue tit at dawn, Walcot Lake; lapwings at Venus Pool.

I am moon-chasing again, and research to see if anyone has ever got a good moonrise over Clun Castle. I think back to the time this ruin was lived in and that those lords and ladies, serfs and villeins would have seen this very moon rise to herald the coming of winter. I am a moonaholic.

One moon is too many and a thousand never enough. I return to Manstone Rock on the Stiperstones on a freezing afternoon. Because I am on a slope below this ancient tor, it is always hard to work out when the moon will finally peek her silver eye over the ridge. It feels like a matter of faith, especially when clouds often spoil the fun at the last second, but I finally get my shot.

Moonrise, Clun Castle; Manstone Rock.

At the end of the month, the sightings of starling murmurations at Whixall Moss in North Shropshire are impossible to resist. This is the first time they have gathered in such large numbers to roost in the willow trees at the edge of this vital nature reserve. I seem to have literally caught the early bird, as there are only a handful of us to witness such grace and spectacle. I have been on safari in Kenya, and to my mind this easily matches the wonders I saw there. The sound is like a great wind coming in and out of focus. Safety in numbers is a very good Darwinian idea and the perfect dusky way to celebrate the majesty of our rural county.

DECEMBER
DULL DAYS WORTH GOING OUT FOR

The cold weather leads to mist hugging the hills, and at dawn I am high on Titterstone Clee Hill, swaddled in a fog that steals both distance and perspective. Such lack of clarity is transformative, rendering the sun into a golden Fabergé ball. The scaffolding on a row of Victorian houses looms like a mythical castle.

This yellow light gives our own village, with the ancient church still at its centre, a pleasing softness that makes me glad we have called it home for the years we brought up our children. We do not have the great storms of the Texas panhandle, but mist chasing up hill and down dale is a worthy pursuit of weather.

In December, even the dull days are worth going out for. When the light falls in the afternoon, red kites begin to gather in Kempton, settling down to roost in a nearby tree. In the early 1990s kites had declined to only twenty pairs hanging on in mid Wales. Recovery has been remarkable except in northern Scotland where, according to the RSPB, many have been poisoned on or around shooting estates. Here in Shropshire, we are entering the first year where there is no need to record numbers as they are so well established.

The great white egret has returned to Walcot Lake, a welcome and rare visitor to this part of the country. A thousand egrets were served at the feast to celebrate the enthronement of the Archbishop of York in 1460. In terms of species decimation, it was all downhill after that. Here is one of few good conservation stories out there as numbers have been increasing and moving north year by year.

We have our first snow of the year and I go out to grab dawn, to see how hill and dale are swathed in a soft bundle of white. Familiar landmarks are rendered strange and the landscape is transformed. A heavy fall of snow and continuing cold temperatures have a remarkable effect on the birds. Their circle of comfort around humans has shrunk. Suddenly, the distant and shy redwing poses for me mere metres away and the thrush, speckled with little imprinted hearts, takes one of those little hearts and sings it right out.

Berries are bejewelled, and the crack gang of blackbird burglars are taking home bright and valuable loot. Even the hare has changed, its shallow 'form' now not a scrape in the earth but a snow hole, as it tucks itself in with flattened ears.

Sunrise on Titterstone Clee Hill; Lydbury North in the mist.

Great white egret, and with heron. [Next pages: a flurry of snow over Lydbury North.]

Feasting blackbird; hare in snow; swan with reflection; a full-throated song thrush; redwing; starling.

My first and only starling deigns to visit our garden. What iridescent glory! What we normally see as a black flash among thousands is here revealed to be quite the fashion icon.

I return with one last hope to Whixall Moss to wait for an aerial spectacle. In the east, the near full moon is soon to rise and when it does, I spot a preening swan in the flooded fields in front of me. Now it's time to focus. Preening will finish and when it does, swan shall flap out its wings and because the water is still, there might also be a reflection to admire.

I pray to the gods of all green goodness and it seems to work as suddenly swan is dancing and the moon looks down with shining approval.

Only then do I turn back round. Dusk falls and groups of starlings begin to gather in the sky, small in number at first and then larger. The rains have done me a huge favour. I clamber over a fence to stand next to a flooded field. Without any wind, this flatness should contain a reflection of all that action building up in the air. Already, the birds are pouring through a funnel, down into their roost in the willow trees, and the floods transform into a perfect mirror. I catch my final shot of December and the result feels more like a painting than a photograph. As I drive back into the night I am content.

I reflect that Shropshire has given me more than I can possibly ever repay. Time itself is the postscript. The winds shall come to scour this memory away; the starlings will disperse. The vast merry-go-round in our little Eden will grind into natural gear again, when holes in trees gain significance with their empty, breezy hollows so suddenly resounding to the chit-chit-chit of hope in this hill and dale.

180   Swan & the moon, Whixall Moss; starling murmuration at Whixall Moss. [Next pages: time-lapse technique shows a great spotted woodpecker leaving the nest in May.]

ANDREW FUSEK PETERS

'I am passionate about capturing light and place, movement and stillness, mainly through landscape, wildlife & garden photography.'

Andrew has twice won Highly Commended in the 'British Wildlife Photographer of the Year', won Commended and Third in Category in 'International Garden Photographer of the Year' and made the top 100 in 'Close-Up Photographer Of The Year'.

His photos appear regularly in the media, including, for example The Guardian, The Observer, The Telegraph, The Sunday Telegraph, The Daily Star, The Sun, The Times, The Sunday Times, The Scotsman, The Daily Mail, The Daily Mirror, The Daily Express, Metro, The Independent, BBC News, Amateur Photographer, Black & White Photography & What Digital Camera and BBC Wildlife Magazine. He has twice made the cover of The Times with his sunset over the Devil's Chair and his supermoon rising over Caer Caradoc. He has had cover shots in Amateur Photographer, EOS Magazine and Olympus Passion. He has had feature pieces in BBC Wildlife, Digital Camera, The Countryman, Country Life, Amateur Photographer, Wild Planet, Birdwatch, Photoplus and EOS Magazine. His 'Hare in the bluebells' was shown on BBC Springwatch Unsprung ('Encapsulates spring,' said Chris Packham.)

As an experienced and entertaining speaker, Andrew regularly gives talks at festivals, conservation groups and camera clubs around the UK and he has appeared at festivals such as Edinburgh, Hay, Althorp and Cheltenham. Andrew has a range of Shropshire 'Wildlife and Landscape' cards available via his website, *www.andrewfusekpeters.com*.

Andrew worked for the National Trust and Natural England on *Stepping Stones*, a project to record species and landscape between the Stiperstones and the Long Mynd. The results were published as a 192-page full-colour book *Upland* by Graffeg. This work led the National Trust to commission him to create the first-ever guidebook for the Long Mynd.

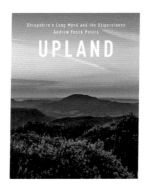

'Upland, by @2peters is a beautiful thing. Published by @graffeg_books it's a testimony to patience and a sharp eye.'
Jackie Morris

'Andrew has created a book full of beautiful, engaging images that take you on a journey into a wilderness full of surprises and characters at every corner. The images alone are jaw-dropping, reminding us all that great exploratory journeys can be made into nature, often in our own overlooked back yard. His passion and enthusiasm absorb you into the very fabric of the habitat and its species. A truly wonderful book that deserves to be on everyone's bookshelf.'
Dr. Richard Shucksmith, British Wildlife Photographer of the Year 2011

Andrew's nature-writing memoir, *Dip*, published by Random House, features his black and white photos. The One Show filmed a feature on Andrew and the book, *You Magazine* did a feature and Andrew was interviewed on R4 Midweek.

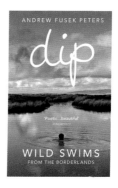

'A poignant memoir'
The Daily Mail.

'A poetic book, the writing is so lyrical and full of metaphor... and there are moments when words and water fuse together'
The Independent.

'A candid, personal and poetic read'
The Scotsman.

'Among the current crop of British nature writers, he deserves a prominent place'
Times Literary Supplement.

'An emerging talent in the world of wildlife photography. His images have a lyrical quality which reflects not only his emotional connection to the natural world but also his heritage as a poet. He presents them with a passion and enthusiasm which are both inspiring and engaging.'
Ben Osborne, Wildlife Photographer Of The Year 2007

INDEX OF PLACES

INDEX OF FLORA & FAUNA

Indexed photographs in italics.

Dust cover photographs: Saddle Rock, Stiperstones (front cover), siskin (inside front flap); female black darter dragonfly at dawn (back cover), kingfisher (inside back flap).

Frontispiece: spotted flycatcher young in a coconut shell. Title page: Lydbury North in mist.

Final page: a spotted flycatcher nesting on the hinge of a busy allotment door leading into the walled garden at Walcot Hall.

On these pages: green woodpecker, male emperor moth

ACKNOWLEDGEMENTS

I would firstly and above all like to thank Philip Rush for the huge amount of time and creative effort he poured into this book, for his faith in my work and for his incredible graphic design skills. *Hill & Dale* could not have happened without him.

Thanks, too, to Fiona Dean for proofreading and fact-checking. Almost certainly, something will have slipped through – but it won't be Fiona's fault!

I am incredibly grateful for the help, support, access and advice I have been freely given by landowners, neighbours, gardeners, old friends and new friends, conservation bodies and farmers. Without you, this book would have simply not been possible. I would like to thank, in no particular order:

Pete Carty, Simon Cooter, Ric Maurice, Lucinda & Robin Parish, Shirley Pennington, Andrew and Barbara Tweedie, Rebecca Burrell, Pete Sagar, Dave Pearce, Stuart Edmunds, Dave Lewis, James Russell, Judith Parish, Kerm, Sue & Phil Wood, Maurice & Jill Phillips, Rachael Kennedy, Diana Walker, Angela Loder-Sykes, Jo Jones, Stephen Barlow, Eric Davies, Steven Roberts, Steve and Ruth Williams, Victoria and Barney, Tom and Gisele Wall, Wendy-Jane Walton, Maxine, Stephen and Lucy Lewis, Angie Hill, Sue at Tea on the Way, Tim Ashton, Alan Reid, Mr and Mrs Cookson, Tris Pearce Wildlife, Terry, Ginny and John Hall.

And huge thanks to my wife Polly, for her patience, encouragement and incredible editorial eye.

ISBN: 9781916375505
© Andrew Fusek Peters, 2020
Published by Yew Tree Press of Stroud.

Yew Tree Press

PRESS & PUBLICATION

January: moon setting over Devil's Chair published in *The Sun*, *Metro* and *Yahoo*. Snowflake on a snowdrop published in *Hereford Times*, *Stourbridge News*, *Powys County Times*, *Worcester News*, *Kidderminster Shuttle*, *Bromsgrove Advertiser*. Goldfinch facing off a chaffinch published in *Digital Camera* magazine. Siskin and goldfinch published in *The Metro* and *Country Life*.

February: Leucistic red kite appeared in *The Countryman*, on the cover of *The Shropshire Star* and in BBC *Wildlife* magazine. Jackdaw against misty sun published in *The Shropshire Star*. Black redstart action sequence first published in *The Daily Telegraph*; frog eye close-up published in *The Daily Telegraph Pictures of the Day*; siskin and blue tit fight published in *The Daily Telegraph* and *Metro*; frogspawn at dusk top 100 finalist Close-Up Photographer of the Year.

March: hare suckling leverets published in *The Daily Telegraph*; little egret in the snow published in *The Countryman*; brook lamprey published in *The Daily Mail* and *The Sun*; great white egret published in *The Shropshire Star*. Star trails above Titterstone Clee published in *The Daily Telegraph Pictures of the Day*; supermoon rising over Manstone Rock published in *The Daily Star*, *The Irish Daily Mirror*, *The Daily Record* and *The Daily Mail*.

April: sparrowhawk taking a collared dove published in *The Times*; kestrel hunting a bumblebee published in *The Times* and *The Shropshire Star*. Robin among the primulas published in *The Yorkshire Post* and *The Daily Telegraph Pictures Of The Day*; blue tit flying the nest published in the *Western Daily Press*; orange-tip butterfly in flight published in *The Scotsman*; dandelion at sunset published in *The Daily Mail Pictures Of The Day* and *The Yorkshire Post*.

May: hare in the bluebells appeared on BBC *Springwatch*; tawny owl chicks at dusk published in *The Times*; sun setting over The Devil's Chair first published on the front page of *The Times*, and on the front of *The Shropshire Star*; woodpecker in flight, published in *The Scotsman*.

June: hare suckling leveret and rabbit attacking hare published in *The Guardian*, *The Sunday Times*, BBC *Wildlife* magazine, *The Countryman*, *The Daily Mail*, *The Times* and *Metro*; blue tit leaving the nest published in *The Daily Telegraph* and *Amateur Photographer*; flycatcher with ringlet published in *The Butterfly Book*, Bloomsbury; robin with worm published in *Polish Newsweek*; cygnet on back of swan published in *The Daily Star*, *The Daily Mail* and *The West Australian*; green woodpecker published in *The Daily Mail* and *Metro*.

July: damselfly at sunset on the Long Mynd published in *The Guardian* and on the front cover of *The Shropshire Star*; Milky Way panorama published in *The Irish Sun* and *The Daily Mail*.

August: dragonfly with dew at dawn published in *The Daily Mail* and *The Daily Telegraph*; the fallow deer that thinks he's a cow published in *The Daily Mail* and *The Daily Telegraph*; black darter at sunset published in *The Daily Mail*; bumblebee on *Echinacea* published on BBC *Newsround* and Commended in International Garden Photographer of the Year 2019; Milky Way over Mitchell's Fold published in *The Daily Mail*.

September: Milky Way over Soulton Long Barrow first published in *The Daily Mail*, *The Guardian* and on the cover of *The Shropshire Star*; wild ponies on the Long Mynd under the harvest moon published in *The Daily Mail*; dawn from Brown Clee Hill published in *The Guardian*; comma in flight published in *Amateur Photographer*.

October: wild pony at dawn on *The Long Mynd* published in *The Sun* and *The Daily Mail*; star trails over Lightspout Waterfall published on the cover of *The Shropshire Star*; leaping salmon at Ashford Carbonel published on the cover of *The Shropshire Star*, in *The Countryman*, and Highly Commended in British Wildlife Photographer of the Year.

November: small tortoiseshell published in *The Observer*; moon over Manstone Rock published in *The Times*; starling murmuration published in *The Times*, *The Daily Telegraph*, *The Independent* and on the cover of *The Shropshire Star*; moon over Clun Castle published in *Digital Camera*.

December: starling murmuration reflection published in *The Western Daily Press*.

Blue tit bringing food for chicks; harvest mouse.